Quotable Elizabeth Warren

Quotable Elizabeth Warren

Edited by
Frank Marshall

Skyhorse Publishing

Skyhorse Publishing books may be purchased in bulk at special discounts for sales promotion, corporate gifts, fund-raising, or educational purposes. Special editions can also be created to specifications. For details, contact the Special Sales Department, Skyhorse Publishing, 307 West 36th Street, 11th Floor, New York, NY 10018 or info@skyhorsepublishing.com.

Skyhorse® and Skyhorse Publishing® are registered trademarks of Skyhorse Publishing, Inc.®, a Delaware corporation.

Visit our website at www.skyhorsepublishing.com.

10 9 8 7 6 5 4 3 2 1

Library of Congress Cataloging-in-Publication Data

Quotable Elizabeth Warren / edited by Frank Marshall.
      pages cm
Summary: "US Senator Elizabeth Warren has long been an original thinker and a powerful voice for the common man. She has been a strong advocate for consumer protection; her work has led to the creation of the US Consumer Financial Protection Bureau. Discover in her own words the woman who has been called "a New Sheriff of Wall Street" by TIME magazine, and "the plainspoken voice of people getting crushed by so many predatory lenders and under regulated banks" by the Boston Globe"— Provided by publisher.
  ISBN 978-1-62914-418-4 (paperback)
  1. Warren, Elizabeth—Political and social views. 2. Women legislators—United States—Quotations. 3. Legislators—United States—Quotations. I. Marshall, Frank.
  E901.1.W37Q67 2014
  081—dc23
                              2014024864
Cover design by Liz Driesbach
Cover photo credit: US Treasury Department
Print ISBN: 978-1-62914-418-4
Ebook ISBN: 978-1-63220-100-3

Printed in the United States of America

Contents

INTRODUCTION

Elizabeth Warren, best known for her roles in politics and academia, is a Democratic US senator from Massachusetts. Prior to her entrance into the political arena, she was a Professor of Law at Harvard University, specializing in bankruptcy and commercial law. Warren has written numerous books and given countless lectures about the current economic climate and what it means for American middleclass families. In her books and lectures, Warren highlights her working class roots and stresses her reluctance to enter the political arena. In *A Fighting Chance*, she writes, "I guess I really can't say that [I am a teacher] anymore. Now I'd have to introduce myself as a United States senator, though I feel a small jolt of surprise whenever I say that." While it is impossible to know how much of Warren's sentiment is hyperbole, she presents herself as a politician out of necessity, passion, and a genuine concern for the American people, not a chosen career path.

The following collection of quotes offers a wide spectrum of the positions Elizabeth Warren has taken during her short tenure as a politician. While she is often criticized and condemned for being *too* liberal or unwavering on her positions, this compilation shows that her wide-ranging ideas actually coalesce into a consistent argument in support of the American middleclass. Surprisingly, Warren supported the Republican Party many years before her political career began, believing that it supported financial growth and independence better than the Democratic alternatives. However, as her interest and knowledge grew in finance, law, and politics, Warren's politics shifted as she came to better understand the reasons behind the exponential financial increase in disparity between rich and poor Americans.

Warren's words shed a clear light on America's past and present, and her ideas for the future offer hope that it is not too late for America to save itself from corporations, corrupt government, and the countless pitfalls that plague this nation.

FRANK MARSHALL

ON GOVERNMENT TRANSPARENCY

There are a lot of regulatory successes, and a lot of people are alive today because of those regulations. But there are still too many places where the world remains complicated and opaque. There are still too many places where armies of lobbyists are fighting to rig the system so that the public remains in the dark.

—*Consumer Federation of America, March 2013*

Putting down rules here and there can be like putting down fence posts on the prairie: They can be too easy to run around. And when the lawyers show everyone how to jog around the fence posts, the regulator responds with more rules. Pretty soon, there are so many rules that it is hard to move.

—*Testimony before the House Financial Services Committee, March 2011*

The boogey man government is like the boogey man under the bed. It is not real. It doesn't exist. What is real and what does exist are all the specific important things we as Americans have chosen to do together through our government.

—Remarks on the Senate Floor, October 2013

If there is a lesson from the past five years, it's this: We all lose when consumers cannot readily determine whether they can afford to pay back their loans, and when lenders sell credit in ways that make it hard to see the risks and costs—in other words, when the system is in some ways fundamentally broken.

—Testimony before the House Financial Services Committee, March 2011

Government agencies work for us,
not for the companies they regulate.
That means agencies should not be
able to cut bad deals and then hide
the embarrassing details. The public
deserves to know what's going on.

—*Blog post, January 2014*

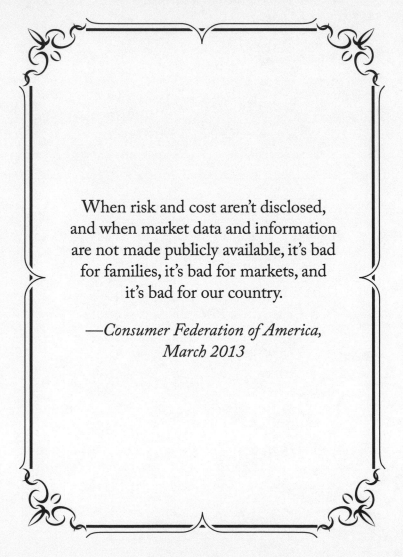

When risk and cost aren't disclosed,
and when market data and information
are not made publicly available, it's bad
for families, it's bad for markets, and
it's bad for our country.

—*Consumer Federation of America,
March 2013*

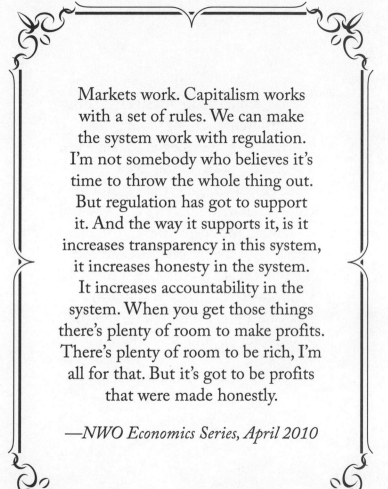

Markets work. Capitalism works with a set of rules. We can make the system work with regulation. I'm not somebody who believes it's time to throw the whole thing out. But regulation has got to support it. And the way it supports it, is it increases transparency in this system, it increases honesty in the system. It increases accountability in the system. When you get those things there's plenty of room to make profits. There's plenty of room to be rich, I'm all for that. But it's got to be profits that were made honestly.

—*NWO Economics Series, April 2010*

By the time the financial crisis hit, a different form of pricing had emerged. Lenders began to use a low advertised price on the front end to entice customers, and then made their real money with fees and charges and penalties and re-pricing in the fine print. Buyers became less and less able to evaluate the risks of a financial product, comparison shopping became almost impossible, and the market became less efficient.

—Americans for Financial Reform and the Roosevelt Institute speech, November 2013

I have heard the argument that transparency would undermine the Trade Representative's policy to complete the trade agreement because public opposition would be significant.

In other words, if people knew what was going on, they would stop it. This argument is exactly backwards. If transparency would lead to widespread public opposition to a trade agreement, then that trade agreement should not be the policy of the United States.

—*Blog post, June 2013*

People want to see action described in terms that make sense to them and that seem fair. They want to see that taxpayer funds aren't being used to shield financial institutions from the consequences of their own actions.

—*Bailout oversight committee hearing, April 2009*

Since when does Congress set deadlines, watch regulators miss most of them, and then take that failure as a reason not to act? I thought that if the regulators failed, it was time for Congress to step in. That's what oversight means. And that's certainly a principle that would have served our country well prior to the crisis.

—Americans for Financial Reform and the Roosevelt Institute speech, November 2013

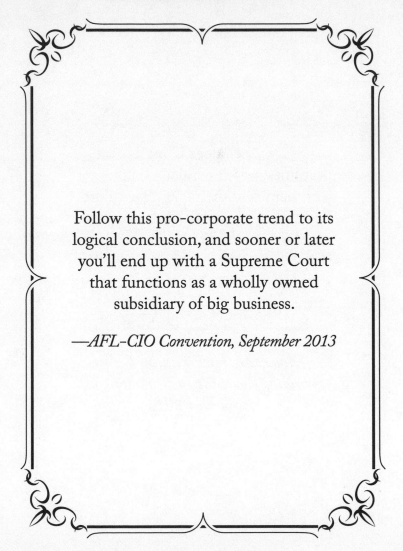

Follow this pro-corporate trend to its logical conclusion, and sooner or later you'll end up with a Supreme Court that functions as a wholly owned subsidiary of big business.

—*AFL-CIO Convention, September 2013*

In granting Treasury such enormous
discretion with TARP money,
Congress expected an equal measure
of transparency and accountability.
Taxpayers have a right to understand
clearly what Treasury is doing, why
it is doing it, what it will accomplish,
and how success will be measured.

*—Congressional Oversight Panel
hearing of Secretary Geithner,
September 2009*

Treasury has not explained how its
financial stabilization programs fit
together to address the problems
that caused this crisis. This failure to
connect specific programs to a clear
strategy aimed at the root causes of the
crisis has produced uncertainty and
drained your work of public support.

—*Open letter to Secretary Geithner,*
March 2009

When you use corporate resources to support think tanks, there are only two possible outcomes from public disclosure—those contributions do not influence the work of the think tanks or those contributions do influence the think tanks' research and conclusions. Either way, shareholders have a right to know how corporate resources are spent, and, even more importantly, policymakers and the public should be aware of your contributions and evaluate the work of the think tanks accordingly.

—Letter to Bank CEOs,
December 2013

What we need is a system that puts an end to the boom and bust cycle. A system that recognizes we don't grow this country from the financial sector; we grow this country from the middle class.

—*Americans for Financial Reform and the Roosevelt Institute speech, November 2013*

Every agency is set up so that the regulators hear over and over from the industry and their lawyers and lobbyists. That means the message is the same over and over—regulate less, do less, create an exception. In building the consumer agency, it was so powerfully important to me to try to set it up structurally so that the people in the agency would hear from real families, from customers of banks. That the wind would blow sometimes from the other direction.

—A Fighting Chance

ON THE FINANCIAL BAILOUT

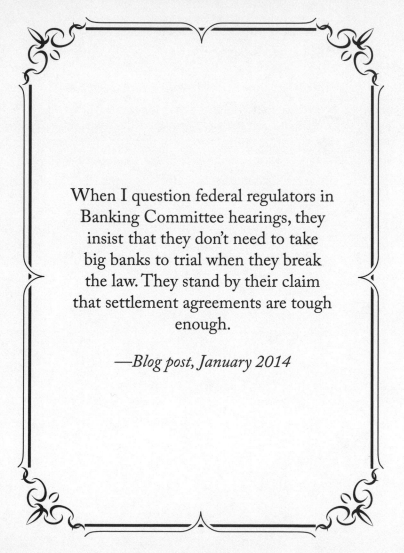

When I question federal regulators in Banking Committee hearings, they insist that they don't need to take big banks to trial when they break the law. They stand by their claim that settlement agreements are tough enough.

—*Blog post, January 2014*

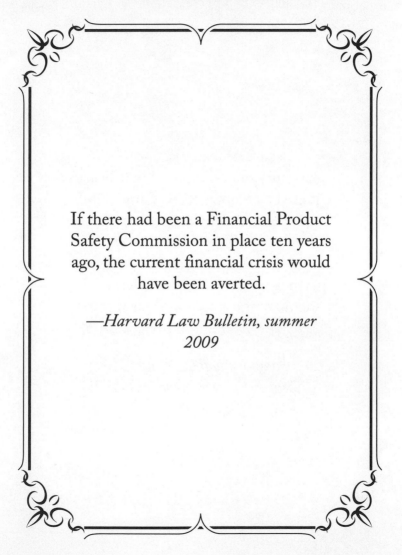

If there had been a Financial Product Safety Commission in place ten years ago, the current financial crisis would have been averted.

—*Harvard Law Bulletin, summer 2009*

The sense of fear and uncertainty has not gone away, but it has been joined by a new sense of anger and frustration. People are angry that even if they have consistently paid their bills on time and never missed a payment, their TARP-assisted banks are unilaterally raising their interest rates or slashing their credit lines.

—Congressional Oversight Panel hearing of Secretary Geithner, April 2009

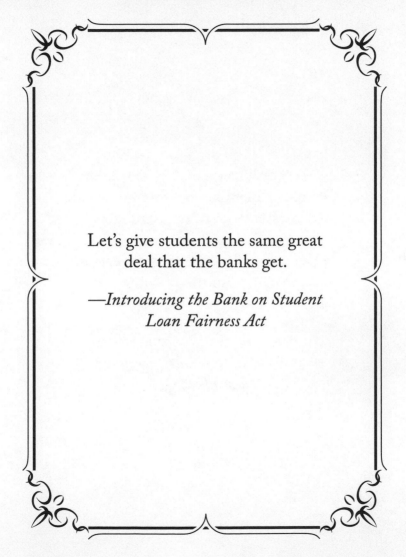

Let's give students the same great
deal that the banks get.

—*Introducing the Bank on Student
Loan Fairness Act*

The crash happened quickly and dramatically, and it caught our nation and apparently even our regulators by surprise. But don't let that fool you. The causes of the crisis were years in the making, and the warning signs were everywhere.

—*Americans for Financial Reform and the Roosevelt Institute speech, November 2013*

People are angry that small businesses are threatened with closure because they can't get financing from their TARP-assisted banks. People are angry that when they read the headlines of record foreclosures, even if they aren't personally affected, they see their own property worth less, and they see their communities declining as a result of the foreclosures around them.

—Congressional Oversight Panel hearing of Secretary Geithner, April 2009

Powerful interests will fight to hang on to every benefit and subsidy they now enjoy. Even after exploiting consumers, larding their books with excessive risk, and making bad bets that brought down the economy and forced taxpayer bailouts, the big Wall Street banks are not chastened. They have fought to delay and hamstring the implementation of financial reform, and they will continue to fight every inch of the way.

—*Americans for Financial Reform and the Roosevelt Institute speech, November 2013*

The rules are the same. Nothing has changed. The laws have not changed. They continue to run their credit rating agencies in the way they believe will best enhance their own profits and revenues. You have to change the rules of the road.

—*NWO Economics Series, April 2010*

People are angry because they are paying for programs that haven't been fully explained and have no apparent benefit for their families or for the economy as a whole, but that seem to leave enough cash in the system for lavish bonuses or golf outings. None of this seems fair.

—Congressional Oversight Panel hearing of Secretary Geithner, April 2009

TARP has become a pejorative four-letter word in the American lexicon. The program is better known across the country as the "Wall Street bailout." Never before has the public been forced to bear the burden of a huge financial wreckage caused by private actors.

—Testimony to the US Senate Committee on Finance, July 2010

A year ago, we were worried about banks that were too big to fail. But in the last year, big banks have gotten bigger, while 84 small banks have been allowed to fail. And some experts are estimating that 1,000 smaller and mid-size banks could disappear before this crisis is over.

I just want to know, are we more at risk on the question of concentration than we were a year ago?

—*Congressional Oversight Panel hearing, September 2010*

Today—that's right, today—marks the fifth anniversary of President Bush signing the bank bailout into law. That financial crisis cost us upwards of $14 trillion. That's trillion with a T. That's $120,000 for every American household, more than two years worth of income for the average family. Billions of dollars in retirement savings disappeared. Millions of workers lost their jobs. And millions more families lost their homes.

—Remarks on the Senate Floor, October 2013

This agency is out here in a sense to try to hold accountable a financial-services industry that ran wild, that brought our economy to the edge of collapse. There's been such a sense that there's one set of rules for trillion-dollar financial institutions and a different set for all the rest of us. It's so pervasive that it's not even hidden.

—Vanity Fair, *November 2011*

Congress is about to write the rules of our economic system that will guide us for the next fifty years. If they get it right we're good. If they get it wrong, the country we knew will be gone. The people need to be on their representatives in Congress and the Senate. This is democracy and if we the people don't insist that those in Washington represent us then they'll go back to the same rules that benefit the large financial institutions. And frankly at that point, we're all just working for the big banks.

—*NWO Economics Series, April 2010*

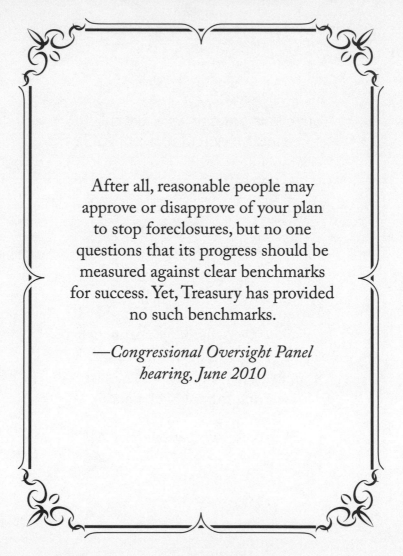

After all, reasonable people may approve or disapprove of your plan to stop foreclosures, but no one questions that its progress should be measured against clear benchmarks for success. Yet, Treasury has provided no such benchmarks.

—*Congressional Oversight Panel hearing, June 2010*

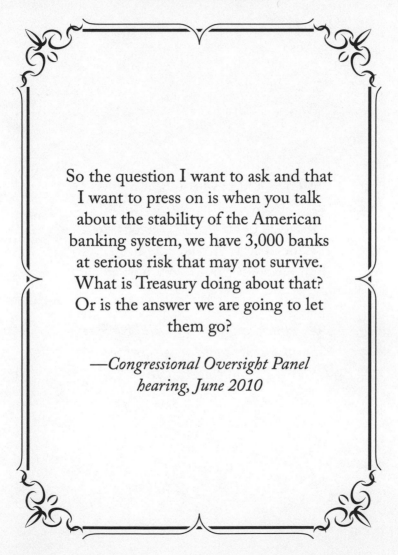

So the question I want to ask and that I want to press on is when you talk about the stability of the American banking system, we have 3,000 banks at serious risk that may not survive. What is Treasury doing about that? Or is the answer we are going to let them go?

—*Congressional Oversight Panel hearing, June 2010*

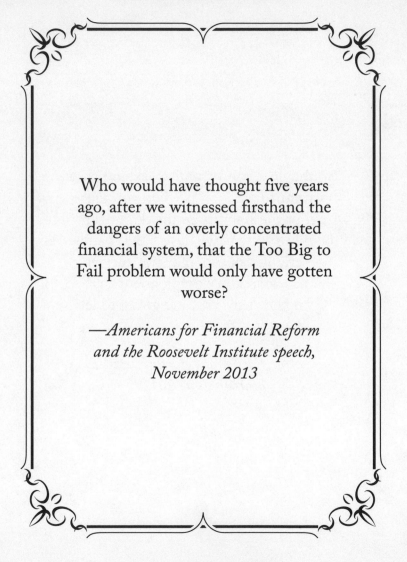

Who would have thought five years ago, after we witnessed firsthand the dangers of an overly concentrated financial system, that the Too Big to Fail problem would only have gotten worse?

—*Americans for Financial Reform and the Roosevelt Institute speech, November 2013*

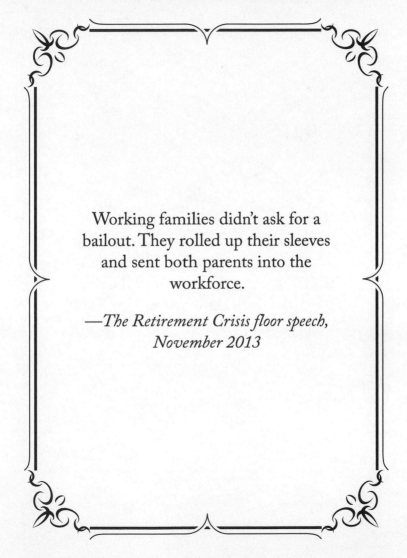

Working families didn't ask for a bailout. They rolled up their sleeves and sent both parents into the workforce.

—*The Retirement Crisis floor speech, November 2013*

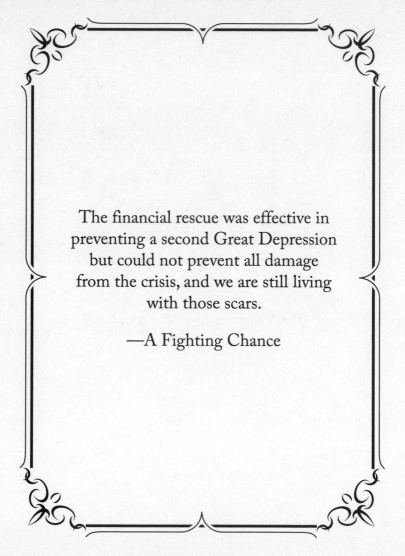

The financial rescue was effective in preventing a second Great Depression but could not prevent all damage from the crisis, and we are still living with those scars.

—A Fighting Chance

ON THE AMERICAN PEOPLE

—⚏—

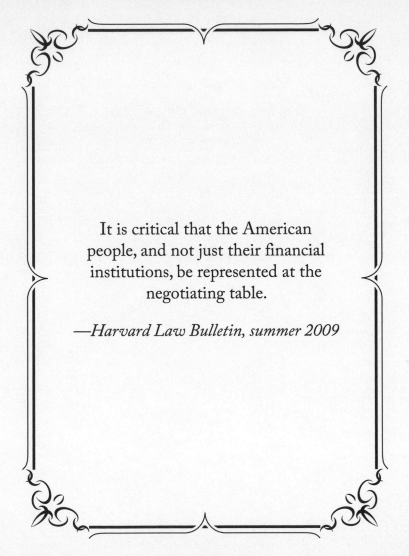

It is critical that the American people, and not just their financial institutions, be represented at the negotiating table.

—*Harvard Law Bulletin, summer 2009*

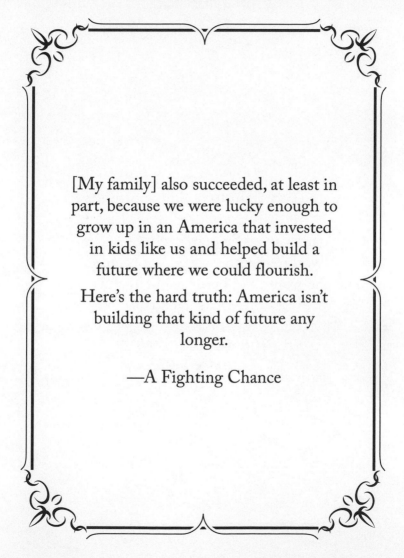

[My family] also succeeded, at least in part, because we were lucky enough to grow up in an America that invested in kids like us and helped build a future where we could flourish.

Here's the hard truth: America isn't building that kind of future any longer.

—A Fighting Chance

In every fight to build opportunity in this country, in every fight to level the playing field, in every fight for working families, we have been on the front lines because our agenda is America's agenda.

—AFL-CIO Convention,
September 2013

The American middle class was forged by families who knew hardship and conflict and who dreamed of giving their children something better. It has survived wars, scandal, epidemics, the Great Depression, and massive transformations in the US economy. It is under assault, but the families that make up the middle are not quitters.

—The Two-Income Trap

For years now, we have heard the claim that America is broke, that we cannot afford to invest in our children and that we must tell our seniors to try to get by on less. We face a world in which those born in wealth will have plenty of opportunity, but those born in poverty have little chance to escape—a world in which people work their hearts out and barely hang on.

That is not the promise of American life. That was not the America of Dr. King's dreams. And that must not be our American future.

—Blog post, January 2014

And I'm appalled that so many Senators cannot admit the simple reality: we are still in the middle of a jobs crisis. People have been looking for work for months or even years. Many are starting to give up entirely. Young people are beginning to think that there isn't a future out there for them. Long-term unemployment isn't just about money; it's also about losing hope.

—Blog post, January 2014

Now, Republicans claim they believe in markets. But as anyone will tell you, a market without rules is not a market; it's the place where the most powerful come to hammer on the least powerful. Progressives understand that markets are like football, that every game needs rules, and the referee blows the whistle to enforce those rules. Without rules and a ref, it isn't football—it's a mugging. That's the big picture, and that's why I'm running for the United States Senate.

—*Remarks to Netroots Nation,*
June 2012

Add all of this up—the dramatic decline in individual savings and the dramatic decline of guaranteed retirement benefits and employer support in return for a lifetime of work—and we're left with a retirement crisis—a crisis that is as real and as frightening as any policy problem facing the United States today.

—*The Retirement Crisis floor speech, November 2013*

And I'm grateful, down to my toes, for every opportunity that America gave me. This is a great country. I grew up in an America that invested in its kids and built a strong middle class; that allowed millions of children to rise from poverty and establish secure lives. An America that created Social Security and Medicare so that seniors could live with dignity; an America in which each generation built something solid so that the next generation could build something better.

—*Democratic National Convention, September 2012*

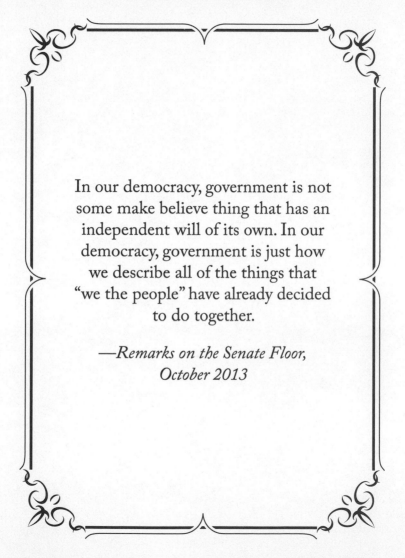

In our democracy, government is not some make believe thing that has an independent will of its own. In our democracy, government is just how we describe all of the things that "we the people" have already decided to do together.

—*Remarks on the Senate Floor, October 2013*

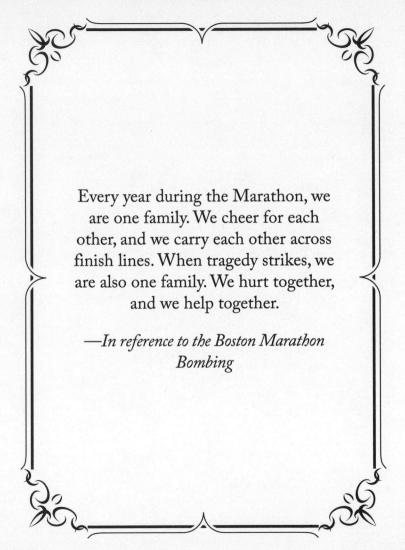

Every year during the Marathon, we are one family. We cheer for each other, and we carry each other across finish lines. When tragedy strikes, we are also one family. We hurt together, and we help together.

—In reference to the Boston Marathon Bombing

Learning from community leaders is not new to me. For years, I have met frequently with such groups, learning about the problems that consumers face in the marketplace and policies that can make a meaningful difference. They have been on the front lines, and the stories they have told often have been harbingers of more system-wide problems to come.

—*Testimony before the House Financial Services Committee, March 2011*

[The American middle class] are ferocious fighters, for themselves and for their children. Their willingness to send twenty million mothers into the workplace had unintended fallout, but it was rooted in a powerful desire to create a better future for their children.

—The Two-Income Trap

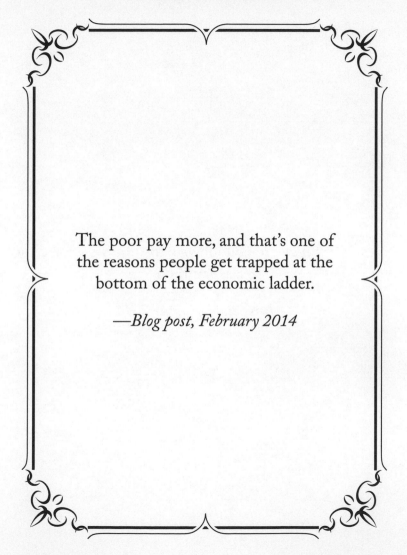

The poor pay more, and that's one of the reasons people get trapped at the bottom of the economic ladder.

—*Blog post, February 2014*

There are no lobbyists for middle-class families.

—Interview, August 2011

As I have traveled back and forth across Massachusetts over the past two years, many people have told me about the challenges they face and their hopes for the future. And every day that I go to the United States Senate I carry those hopes, along with a determination to give families a fighting chance.

—*Blog post, August 2013*

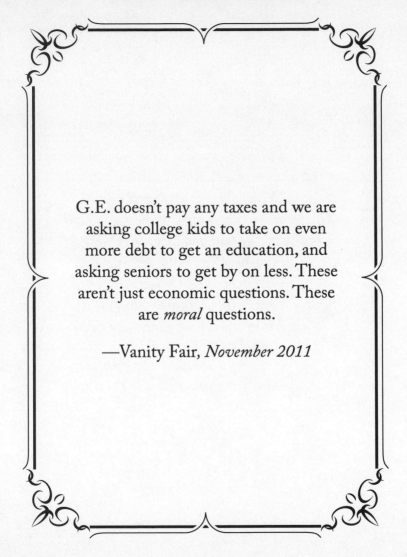

G.E. doesn't pay any taxes and we are asking college kids to take on even more debt to get an education, and asking seniors to get by on less. These aren't just economic questions. These are *moral* questions.

—Vanity Fair, *November 2011*

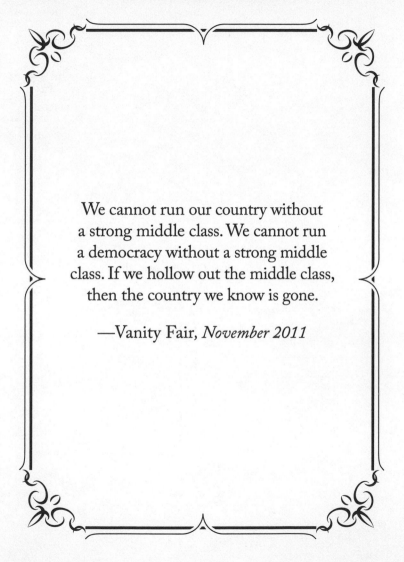

We cannot run our country without a strong middle class. We cannot run a democracy without a strong middle class. If we hollow out the middle class, then the country we know is gone.

—Vanity Fair, *November 2011*

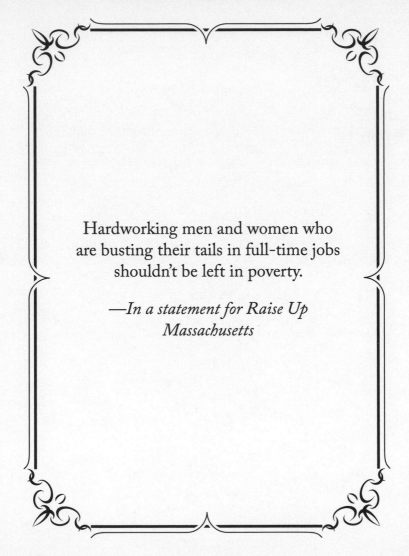

Hardworking men and women who are busting their tails in full-time jobs shouldn't be left in poverty.

—*In a statement for Raise Up Massachusetts*

Americans are fighters. We're tough, resourceful and creative, and if we have the chance to fight on a level playing field, where everyone pays a fair share and everyone has a real shot, then no one—no one can stop us.

—*Democratic National Convention, September 2012*

We are a nation of innovators and entrepreneurs, growing small businesses and thriving big businesses. But our people succeed—our country succeeds—because we have all come together to put public institutions and infrastructure together.

—*Remarks on the Senate Floor, October 2013*

If we started in 1960, and we said that as productivity goes up, then the minimum wage is going to go up the same. If that were the case, the minimum wage today would be about $22 an hour. . . . So my question is, what happened to the other $14.75?

—*Senate Committee on Health, Education, Labor, and Pensions hearing*

Labor was on the front lines to take children out of factories and put them in schools. Labor was there to give meaning to the words "consumer protection" by making our food and medicine safe. Labor was there to fight for minimum wages in states across this country.

—*AFL-CIO Convention, September 2013*

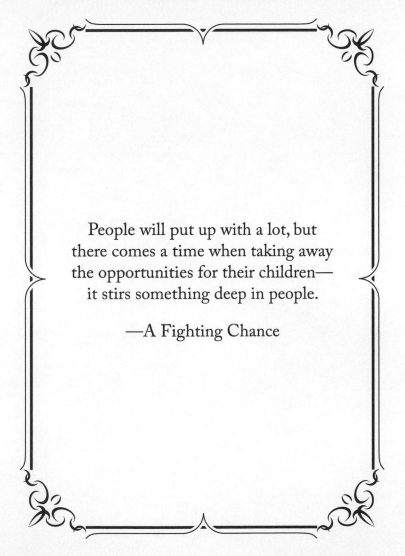

People will put up with a lot, but there comes a time when taking away the opportunities for their children— it stirs something deep in people.

—A Fighting Chance

On Corporatism in Washington

—◊—

You built a factory out there? Good for you. But I want to be clear: you moved your goods to market on the roads the rest of us paid for; you hired workers the rest of us paid to educate; you were safe in your factory because of police forces and fire forces that the rest of us paid for. You didn't have to worry that marauding bands would come and seize everything at your factory, and hire someone to protect against this, because of the work the rest of us did.

—*CBS News, September 2011*

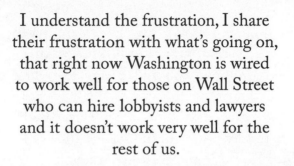

I understand the frustration, I share their frustration with what's going on, that right now Washington is wired to work well for those on Wall Street who can hire lobbyists and lawyers and it doesn't work very well for the rest of us.

—In reference to the Occupy Wall Street Movement, October 2011

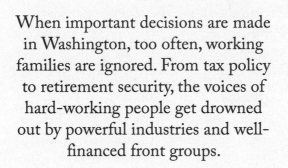

When important decisions are made in Washington, too often, working families are ignored. From tax policy to retirement security, the voices of hard-working people get drowned out by powerful industries and well-financed front groups.

—*Our Agenda Is America's Agenda speech*

Here in Washington, power is not balanced. Instead, power is becoming more concentrated on one side. There are powerful, deep-pocketed corporate interests lined up to fight to protect their privilege and to resist any change that would limit corporate excesses.

—*Speech to the American Constitution Society, June 2013*

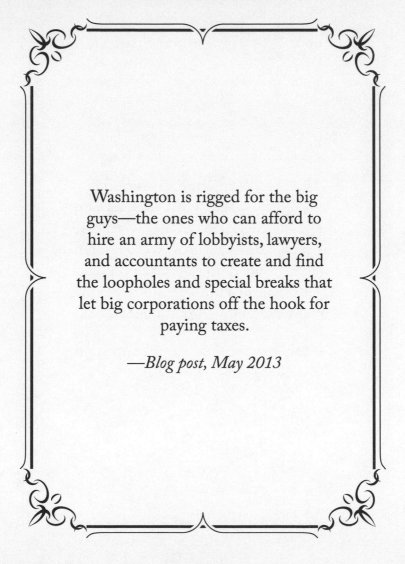

Washington is rigged for the big guys—the ones who can afford to hire an army of lobbyists, lawyers, and accountants to create and find the loopholes and special breaks that let big corporations off the hook for paying taxes.

—Blog post, May 2013

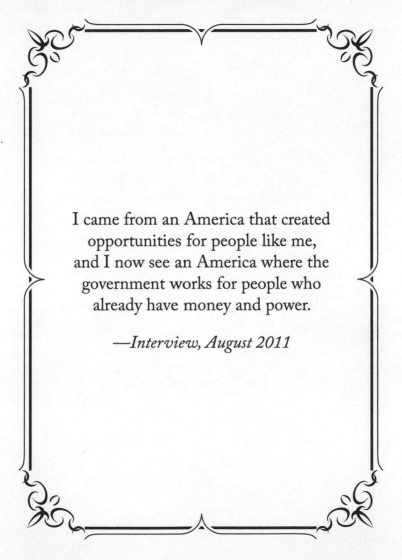

I came from an America that created opportunities for people like me, and I now see an America where the government works for people who already have money and power.

—*Interview, August 2011*

Big corporations hire armies of
lobbyists to get billion-dollar
loopholes into the tax system and
persuade their friends in Congress to
support laws that keep the playing
field tilted in their favor. Meanwhile,
hardworking families are told that
they'll just have to live with smaller
dreams for their children.

—A Fighting Chance

Now look, you built a factory and it turned into something terrific, or a great idea? God bless. Keep a big hunk of it. But part of the underlying social contract is you take a hunk of that and pay forward for the next kid who comes along.

—*CBS News, September 2011*

According to a recent study, the five conservative justices currently sitting on the Supreme Court are in the top ten most pro-corporate justices in a half century—and Justices Alito and Roberts are numbers one and two—the most anti-consumer in this entire time. The Chamber of Commerce is now a major player in the Supreme Court, and its win rate has risen to 70% of all cases it supports.

—*Our Agenda Is America's Agenda speech*

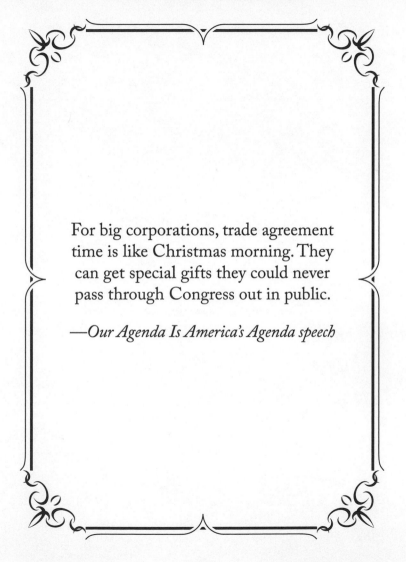

For big corporations, trade agreement time is like Christmas morning. They can get special gifts they could never pass through Congress out in public.

—*Our Agenda Is America's Agenda speech*

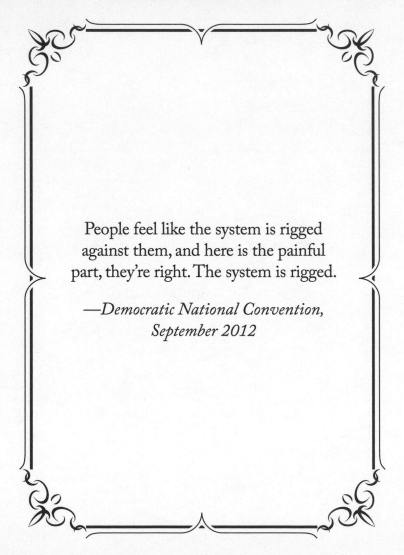

People feel like the system is rigged against them, and here is the painful part, they're right. The system is rigged.

—*Democratic National Convention, September 2012*

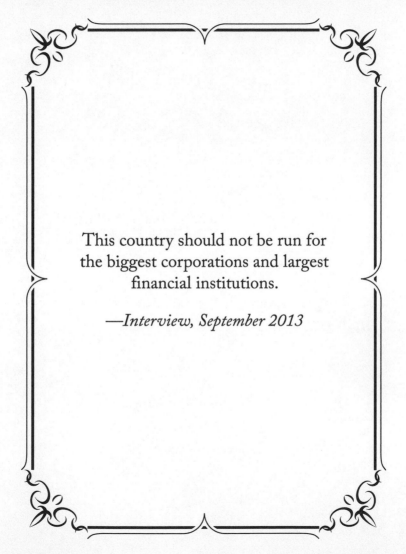

This country should not be run for
the biggest corporations and largest
financial institutions.

—*Interview, September 2013*

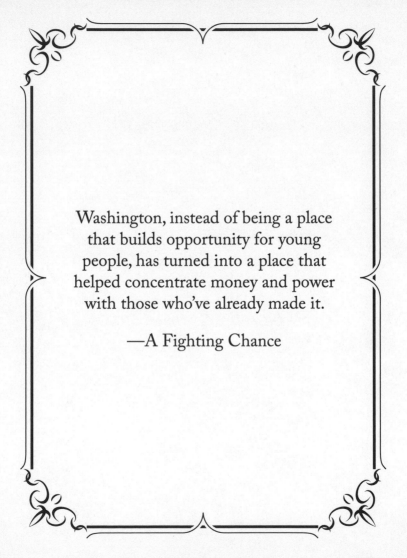

Washington, instead of being a place that builds opportunity for young people, has turned into a place that helped concentrate money and power with those who've already made it.

—A Fighting Chance

Look around. Oil companies guzzle down the billions in profits. Billionaires pay a lower tax rate than their secretaries, and Wall Street CEOs—the same ones who wrecked our economy and destroyed millions of jobs—still strut around Congress, no shame, demanding favors, and acting like we should thank them. Anyone here have a problem with that?

—*Democratic National Convention, September 2012*

On the American Right

I don't kid myself. Fighting back isn't easy. Powerful interests invested in the status quo know what is at stake. They are organized, they are effective, and they come to this battle with armies of lobbyists and lawyers. We are up against a conservative movement that for thirty years—since President Reagan—has dedicated itself to packing the courts with pro-business, anti-regulation, conservative allies. They are tough and they are prepared.

—*Speech to the American Constitution Society, June 2013*

For years now we have heard a small minority in this country rail against government. When I hear the latest tirades from some of the extremists in the House, I am struck by how vague these complaints are. From their rhetoric, you'd think they believed that anytime "We the People" come together to improve our lives, the nation is committing some terrible wrong. From their rhetoric, you'd think they believe that the government that functions best is a government that doesn't function at all. So far, they haven't ended government, but they have achieved the next best thing—shutting the government down.

—*On the 2013 Government Sequester, October 2013*

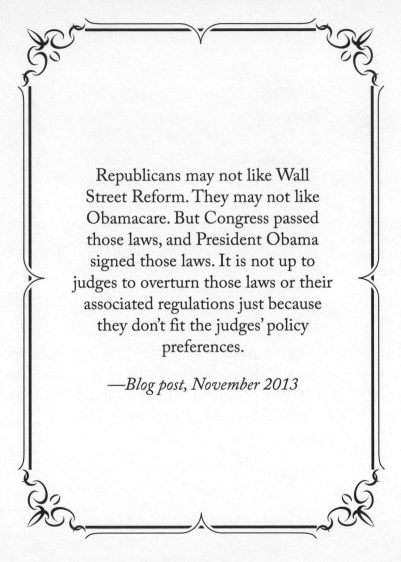

Republicans may not like Wall Street Reform. They may not like Obamacare. But Congress passed those laws, and President Obama signed those laws. It is not up to judges to overturn those laws or their associated regulations just because they don't fit the judges' policy preferences.

—*Blog post, November 2013*

The political minority in the House that condemns government and begged for this shutdown has its day. But like all the reckless and extremist factions that have come before it, its day will pass—and the government will get back to the work we have chosen to do together.

—*Blog post, October 2013*

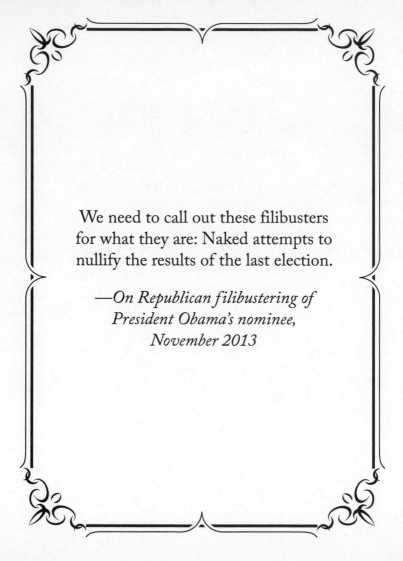

We need to call out these filibusters for what they are: Naked attempts to nullify the results of the last election.

—On Republican filibustering of President Obama's nominee, November 2013

I'm out there working for Jamie Dimon the same way Dick Cheney is out there trying to save the environment.

—On accusations that she wants to increase Social Security benefits of billionaires

Nearly one million federal employees are sitting at home for no reason, and other public servants are working but not earning a paycheck. Cancer patients are being turned away from clinical trials at the NIH. Veterans' benefits are at risk. Basic nutrition services for pregnant women and new moms will be disrupted. Small businesses won't be able to get federal loan guarantees.

—On the 2013 Government Sequester, October 2013

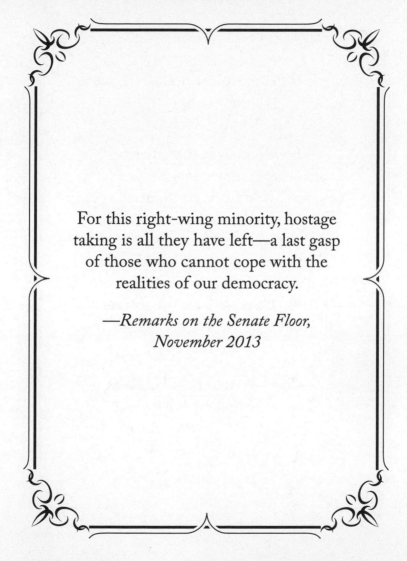

For this right-wing minority, hostage taking is all they have left—a last gasp of those who cannot cope with the realities of our democracy.

—*Remarks on the Senate Floor, November 2013*

Mitt Romney is the guy who said corporations are people. No, Governor Romney, corporations are not people. People have hearts, they have kids, they get jobs, they get sick, they cry, they dance. They live, they love, and they die. And that matters. That matters because we don't run this country for corporations, we run it for people.

—Remarks on the Senate Floor, November 2013

The American people don't want the extremist Republican's bizarre vision of a future without government. They don't support it. Why? Because the American people know that without government, we would no longer be a great nation with a bright future. The American people know that government matters.

—*Remarks on the Senate Floor, November 2013*

The fight continues to rage, and the powerful interests continue to be guided by their age-old principle: "I've got mine, the rest of you are on your own." But we're guided by principle too. It's a simple idea, and all of you know it as an old labor idea—we all do better when we work together and invest in our future.

—AFL-CIO Convention, September 2013

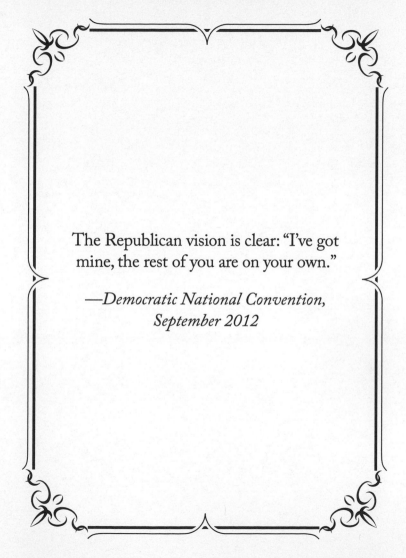

The Republican vision is clear: "I've got mine, the rest of you are on your own."

—*Democratic National Convention,*
September 2012

ON BECOMING A BETTER AMERICA

—ɯ—

Here's what haunts my dreams, I
wake up, at 5 in the morning, fearing
that it's a year from now, and things
have not gone well, and I missed
something. Maybe I failed to identify
the critical link that we should have
looked at, or failed to say something
urgently enough to someone in power,
or failed to explain with enough
clarity that the American people
could understand why they needed
to support something or needed to
attack it. I worry that a year from now
I will understand how I fell short.
And all I can do now is my best, but I
don't know if I'll get it right. I will try.

—*Harvard Law Bulletin,*
summer 2009

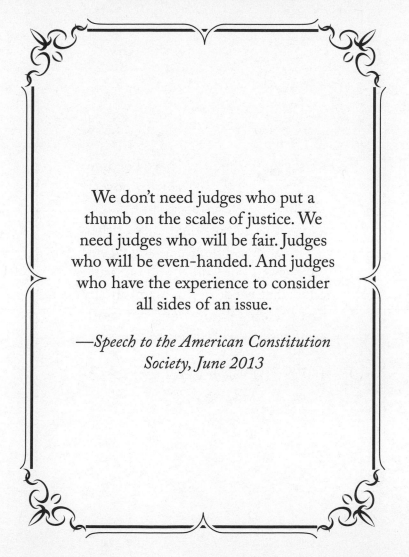

We don't need judges who put a thumb on the scales of justice. We need judges who will be fair. Judges who will be even-handed. And judges who have the experience to consider all sides of an issue.

—*Speech to the American Constitution Society, June 2013*

The suggestion that we have become a country where those living in poverty fight each other for a handful of crumbs tossed off the tables of the very wealthy is fundamentally wrong. This is about our values, and our values tell us that we don't build a future by first deciding who among our most vulnerable will be left to starve.

—*The Retirement Crisis floor speech, November 2013*

In measuring progress, as well as
in assessing the current state of
the economy and institutions, we
shouldn't be afraid of facts. There may
be initial pain as the market reacts
and reprices, but the short-term pain
is better than the problems we face
with ongoing uncertainty
and mistrust.

*—Congressional Oversight Panel
hearing of Secretary Geithner,
April 2009*

Mister President, the conversation about retirement and Social Security benefits is not just a conversation about math. At its core, this is a conversation about our values. It is a conversation about who we are as a country and who we are as a people.

—*The Retirement Crisis floor speech, November 2013*

So these proposals, they'll require some big changes. And getting our system right will take sacrifice: sacrifice from Congress, from the states, and from the colleges themselves; but the way we build a future for our children, will be the measure of who we are as a people.

—Remarks to the Education Writers Association Conference on Higher Education

Now is the time to rebuild America's middle class. Instead of giving tax breaks to the already-rich and already-powerful, to the corporations and CEOs who have already made it, it's time America recognized the working people and small businesses who are still trying to build a future.

—elizabethwarren.com, "Priorities"

We know that government doesn't always work. We know that no institution is infallible. People make mistakes, ideas fail, and sometimes we get things wrong. But our response isn't to give up. Our response isn't to sit back and say: I told you so. We aren't a nation of quitters. Our response, the American response, is to fix it, to make government work better.

—Remarks on the Senate Floor,
October 2013

We need to make it easier for workers who want to organize to have the chance to do so. If people want to work together for better wages, for better health care, and for better working conditions, they should have the right to do so.

—elizabethwarren.com, "Jobs & The Economy"

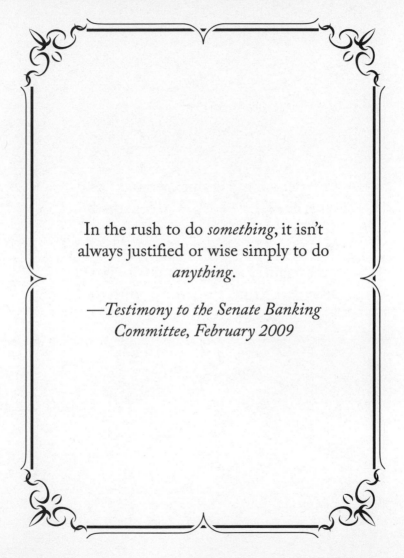

In the rush to do *something*, it isn't always justified or wise simply to do *anything*.

—*Testimony to the Senate Banking Committee, February 2009*

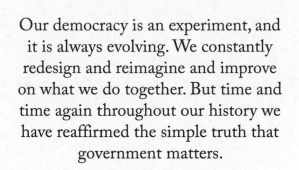

Our democracy is an experiment, and it is always evolving. We constantly redesign and reimagine and improve on what we do together. But time and time again throughout our history we have reaffirmed the simple truth that government matters.

—*Remarks on the Senate Floor,*
November 2013

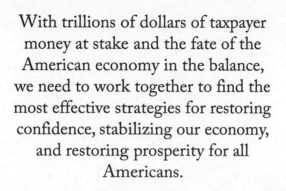

With trillions of dollars of taxpayer money at stake and the fate of the American economy in the balance, we need to work together to find the most effective strategies for restoring confidence, stabilizing our economy, and restoring prosperity for all Americans.

—*Congressional Oversight Panel hearing of Secretary Geithner, April 2009*

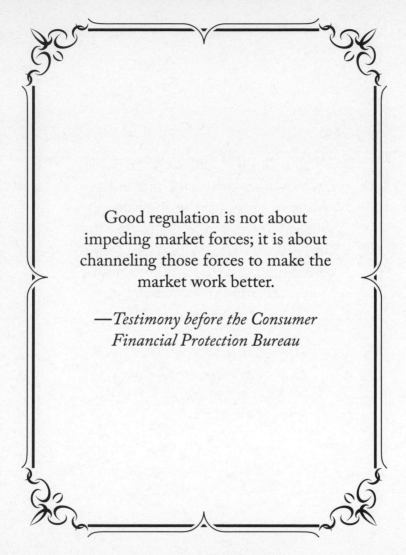

Good regulation is not about impeding market forces; it is about channeling those forces to make the market work better.

—*Testimony before the Consumer Financial Protection Bureau*

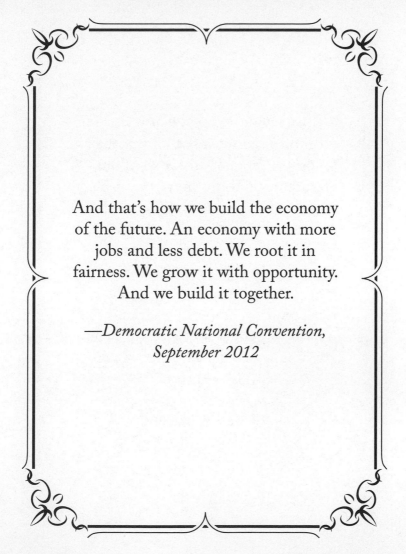

And that's how we build the economy of the future. An economy with more jobs and less debt. We root it in fairness. We grow it with opportunity. And we build it together.

—*Democratic National Convention, September 2012*

If we invest now in twenty-first-century energy, we can lower the costs of production for all of our future work. Right now, renewable energy competes with old energies that get lots of special breaks in Washington. Massachusetts can lead the world in using green technology to cut production costs and make our products competitive around the world. We could do this right here, right now—and create jobs here in Massachusetts.

—elizabethwarren.com,
"Energy & The Environment"

[One] vision of how America works is that it's an even game, that anybody can get started—just roll those dice; that booms and busts will come and millions of people will lose their homes, millions more will lose their jobs, and trillions of dollars in savings retirement accounts will be wiped out. The question is, do we have a different vision of what we can do?

—Vanity Fair, *November 2011*

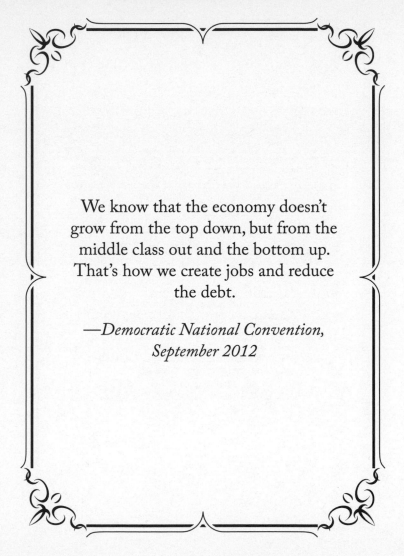

We know that the economy doesn't grow from the top down, but from the middle class out and the bottom up. That's how we create jobs and reduce the debt.

—Democratic National Convention, September 2012

The Food and Drug Administration makes sure that the white pills that we take are antibiotics and not baking soda. The National Highway Traffic Safety Administration oversees crash tests to make sure that all new cars have effective brakes. The Consumer Product Safety Commission makes sure that babies' car seats don't collapse in a crash and the toasters don't explode. We don't know who they are. But there is no question that there are Americans alive today, Americans who are healthier, Americans who are stronger because of these and countless other government efforts. Alive, healthier, stronger because of what we did together.

—*Remarks on the Senate Floor, October 2013*

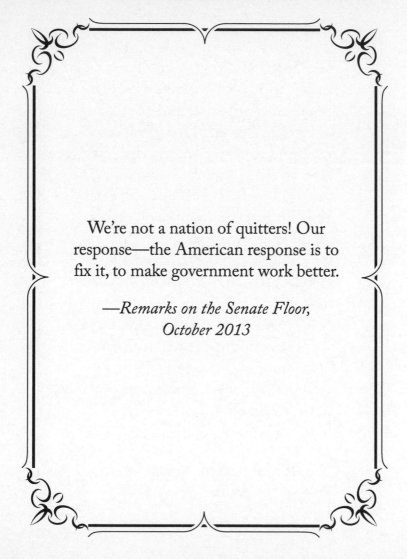

We're not a nation of quitters! Our response—the American response is to fix it, to make government work better.

—*Remarks on the Senate Floor, October 2013*

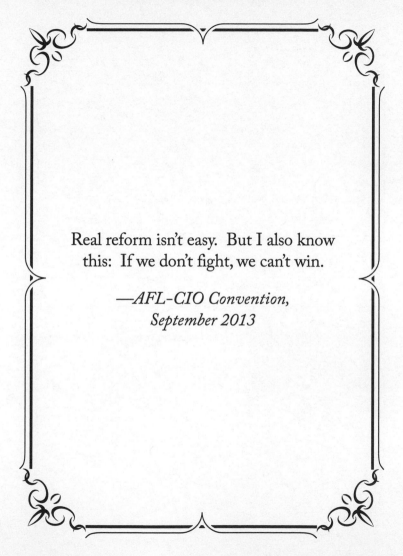

Real reform isn't easy. But I also know
this: If we don't fight, we can't win.

—*AFL-CIO Convention,*
September 2013

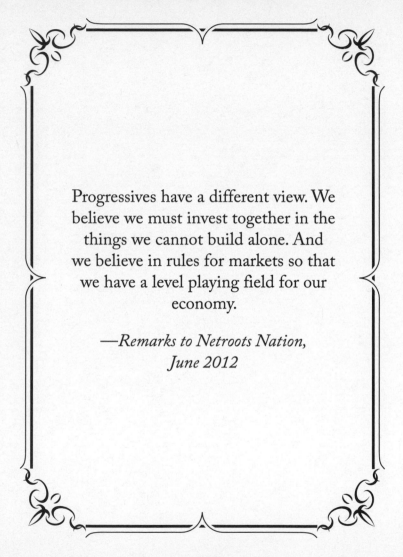

Progressives have a different view. We believe we must invest together in the things we cannot build alone. And we believe in rules for markets so that we have a level playing field for our economy.

—*Remarks to Netroots Nation,*
June 2012

ON WALL STREET

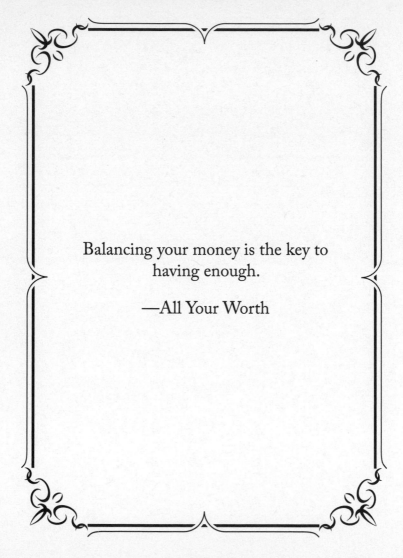

Balancing your money is the key to
having enough.

—All Your Worth

But if a settlement is so weak that Wall Street is celebrating with pay raises, it's not a good deal for the American people.

—*Blog post, January 2014*

Our self-employed and small businesses, and the community banks that fund them, are drowning in complicated regulations. Long, complex rules create loopholes that the big companies can take advantage of, but they leave little guys out in the cold. We need rules that are written with small businesses in mind. We need straightforward rules that any small business can deal with, like the short and streamlined mortgage form the consumer agency is putting into law.

—*elizabethwarren.com,*
"Jobs & The Economy"

We should never forget the consequences of letting financial behemoths hold our economy hostage. Exactly five years ago, our economy seemed to be hurtling toward another Great Depression. We managed to avoid that grim fate, but our economy still suffered a staggering body-blow.

—*The* Boston Globe, *September 2013*

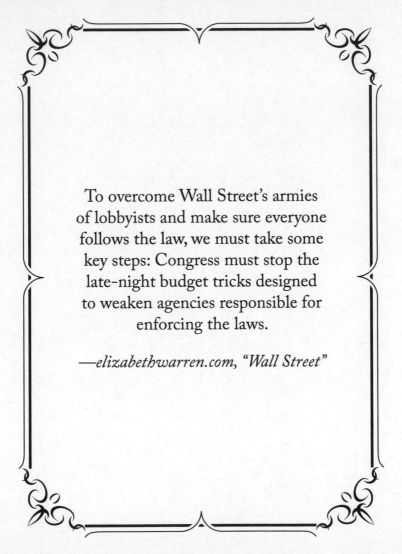

To overcome Wall Street's armies of lobbyists and make sure everyone follows the law, we must take some key steps: Congress must stop the late-night budget tricks designed to weaken agencies responsible for enforcing the laws.

—*elizabethwarren.com, "Wall Street"*

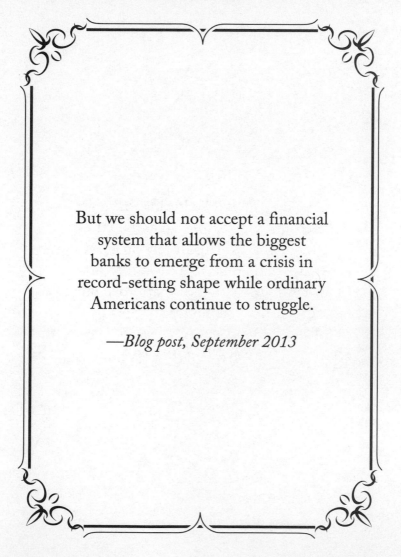

But we should not accept a financial system that allows the biggest banks to emerge from a crisis in record-setting shape while ordinary Americans continue to struggle.

—*Blog post, September 2013*

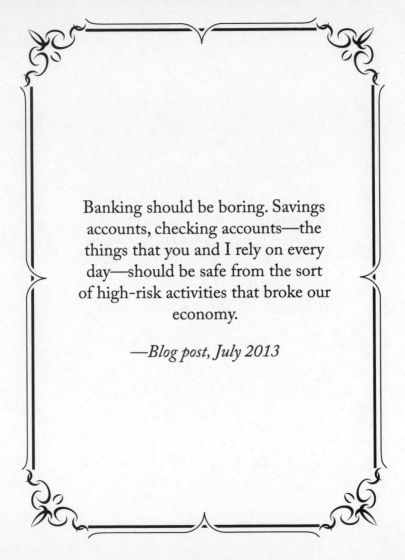

Banking should be boring. Savings accounts, checking accounts—the things that you and I rely on every day—should be safe from the sort of high-risk activities that broke our economy.

—*Blog post, July 2013*

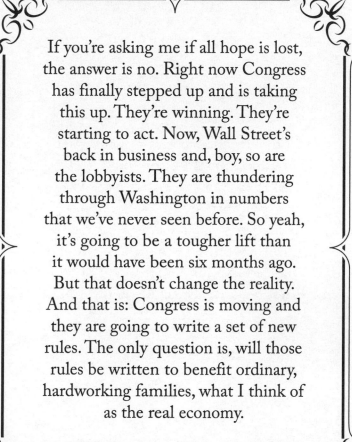

If you're asking me if all hope is lost, the answer is no. Right now Congress has finally stepped up and is taking this up. They're winning. They're starting to act. Now, Wall Street's back in business and, boy, so are the lobbyists. They are thundering through Washington in numbers that we've never seen before. So yeah, it's going to be a tougher lift than it would have been six months ago. But that doesn't change the reality. And that is: Congress is moving and they are going to write a set of new rules. The only question is, will those rules be written to benefit ordinary, hardworking families, what I think of as the real economy.

—NWO Economics Series, April 2010

I do not understand how it is that financial institutions could think that they could take taxpayer money and then turn around and act like it's business as usual. I don't understand how they can't see that the world has changed in a fundamental way, that it is not business as usual when you take taxpayer dollars.

—*Interview, October 2009*

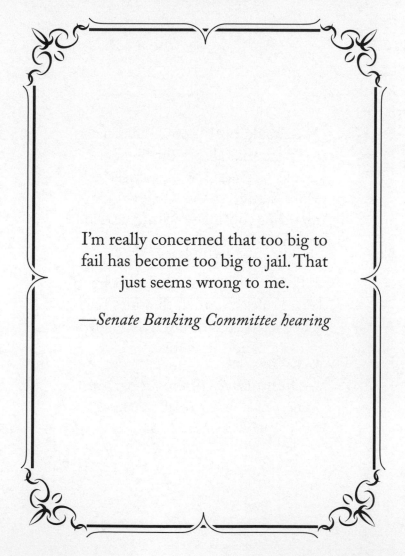

I'm really concerned that too big to fail has become too big to jail. That just seems wrong to me.

—*Senate Banking Committee hearing*

We should not accept a financial system that allows the biggest banks to emerge from a crisis in record-setting shape while working Americans continue to struggle. And we should not accept a regulatory system that is so besieged by lobbyists for the big banks that it takes years to deliver rules and then the rules that are delivered are often watered-down and ineffective.

—*Americans for Financial Reform and the Roosevelt Institute speech, November 2013*

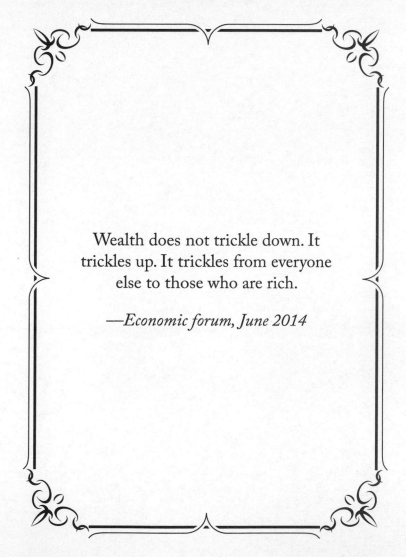

Wealth does not trickle down. It
trickles up. It trickles from everyone
else to those who are rich.

—*Economic forum, June 2014*

ON HEALTH CARE

—⚏—

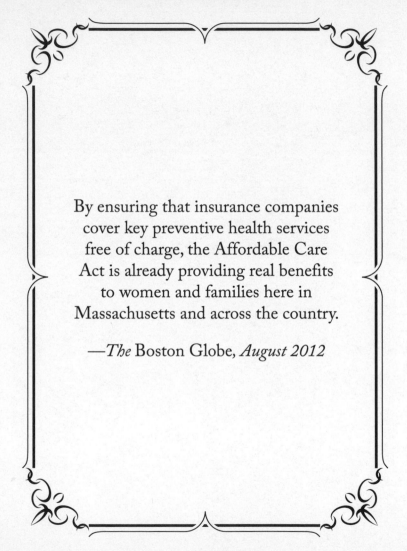

By ensuring that insurance companies cover key preventive health services free of charge, the Affordable Care Act is already providing real benefits to women and families here in Massachusetts and across the country.

—*The* Boston Globe, *August 2012*

Health insurance isn't an on-off switch, giving full protection to everyone who has it. There is real coverage and there is faux coverage. Policies that can be canceled when you need them most are often useless. So is bare-bones coverage like the Utah Medicaid program pioneered by new Health and Human Services Secretary Mike Leavitt; it pays for primary care visits but not specialists or hospital care. We need to talk about quality, durable coverage, not just about how to get more names listed on nearly-useless insurance policies.

—*The* Washington Post,
February 2005

I support the Affordable Care Act. Thanks to the new law, insurance companies cannot discriminate based on pre-existing conditions, 2.5 million young adults are now covered by health insurance through their parents' plan and more than 100 million people no longer have a lifetime limit on their insurance. Going forward, Congress should focus more on lowering costs. That's what I'll do as a US Senator.

—*Masslive.com, March 2012*

Nobody's safe. Health insurance? That didn't protect one million Americans who were financially ruined by illness or medical bills last year.

—*The* Washington Post,
February 2005

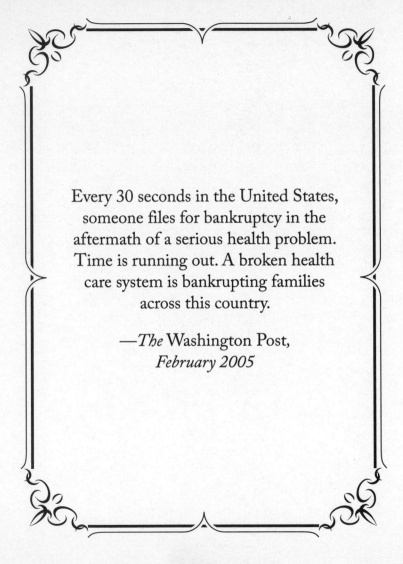

Every 30 seconds in the United States, someone files for bankruptcy in the aftermath of a serious health problem. Time is running out. A broken health care system is bankrupting families across this country.

—*The* Washington Post, *February 2005*

We approach the health care debates from a single perspective: maintaining the financial stability of families confronting illness or injury. The most obvious solution would be universal single-payer health care.

—*Health at Risk,* "Get Sick, Go Broke," coauthored with Deborah Thorne

I cannot believe that we live in a world where we would even *consider* letting some big corporation deny the women who work for it access to the basic medical tests, treatments or prescriptions that they need based on vague moral objections.

—*Blog post, March 2014*

Federal policy is now moving in the right direction: The new health care reform law will soon ban abusive insurance company practices, and it will no longer be the case that simply being a woman, being pregnant, or being a victim of domestic violence is a pre-existing condition that could limit access to coverage. These are powerful protections that women across this country will soon enjoy— if those who want to repeal health care reforms do not succeed. These protections are fundamental, and we owe it to women all across this country to fight to preserve these protections.

—elizabethwarren.com, "Women's Health Issues"

On Other Key Issues

Good public schools, good public universities, and good technical training can give us a workforce better than any in the world. Well-trained workers are cost effective, and they can give us a powerful competitive advantage in world markets. Investments in our people pay the highest dividends.

—*elizabethwarren.com*, *"Education"*

Fair trade: If we are going to sell our products to the rest of the world, we need to strengthen trade laws and ensure their enforcement. We need to make sure that those we compete with also respect workers' rights and environmental rules.

—*elizabethwarren.com, "Priorities"*

We need a twenty-first-century
manufacturing base and expanded
service capacity. We need a set of
workable rules that don't tangle
up those who are trying to create
something new. We need to be able
to invent things, make things, and sell
things to the rest of the world. We
did that once, and we can do it again.

—elizabethwarren.com, "Priorities"

There is a huge difference between the guns of a sportsman or homeowner and high-powered assault weapons with 100-cartridge magazines. I grew up around guns and gun owners, and I will work to protect the rights of law-abiding citizens. But the law must reflect the reality that, in the wrong hands, guns can be used for violent crimes, making neighborhoods less safe.

—*The* Boston Globe, *July 2012*

Too many have been using scare tactics when it comes to Social Security. Social Security can pay 100% of benefits for at least the next twenty years. Instead of taking on special interests, too many politicians have proposed privatizing Medicare, turning it into a voucher program, or cutting it altogether. I will not support privatizing Medicare, turning it into a voucher program, or cutting benefits.

—*The* Boston Globe, *July 2012*

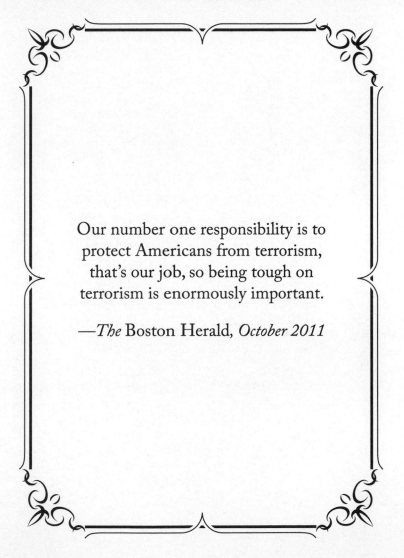

Our number one responsibility is to protect Americans from terrorism, that's our job, so being tough on terrorism is enormously important.

—*The* Boston Herald, *October 2011*

The United States must take the necessary steps to prevent Iran from acquiring a nuclear weapon. I support strong sanctions against Iran and believe that the United States must also continue to take a leadership role in pushing other countries to implement strong sanctions as well. Iran must not have an escape hatch.

—*elizabethwarren.com, "Foreign Policy"*

These threats are not going away. We must remain vigilant. Al Qaeda has operations or affiliates in Pakistan, Yemen, Somalia, and elsewhere around the world. We need to continue our aggressive efforts against Al Qaeda, and we need to continue to support the efforts of our intelligence, law enforcement, homeland security, and military professionals.

—*CounterPunch, October 2012*

We can't stay and rebuild Afghanistan forever. I think it is time to bring our troops home.

—Fox News, October 2012

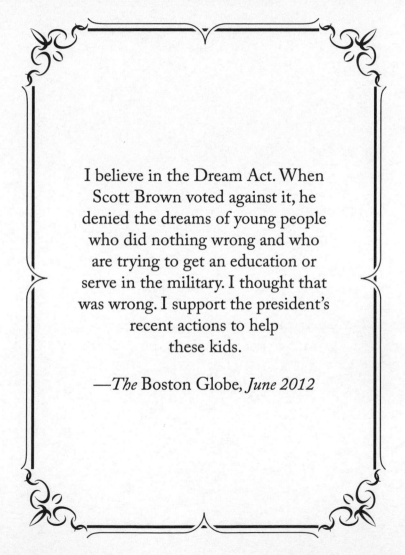

I believe in the Dream Act. When Scott Brown voted against it, he denied the dreams of young people who did nothing wrong and who are trying to get an education or serve in the military. I thought that was wrong. I support the president's recent actions to help these kids.

—*The* Boston Globe, *June 2012*

I think there's a real question about whether or not this "Secure Communities" bill really makes communities more secure. If people feel like they can't go to the police, that doesn't make us more secure. I think we really have to think much harder about the ways to make American communities more secure.

—*Treehugger.com, December 2011*

Most independent deficit analysts say entitlement projected spending will need to be reduced to solve the budget deficit. We should start there before we even consider breaking the promises we made to our seniors. It would be a breach of trust—and just plain poor economic policy— to jeopardize these programs with unnecessary cuts or risky privatization schemes, especially when the wealthy and well-connected continue to enjoy special tax deals.

—*The* Boston Globe, *July 2012*

Social Security is safe for at least
the next twenty years and, if we act
quickly, we can make modest changes
that will keep the system solvent
without cutting back on benefits. We
need honesty and political will to
move forward.

—*elizabethwarren.com, "Social Security"*

We need to upgrade our aging roads,
bridges, mass transit, and water and
sewage lines—the basic pieces it takes
to manufacture goods and to get them
to market. My brother-in-law Steve
operates a Gradall out of Plymouth.
He tells me that he digs up water and
sewage pipes in some parts of the
state that were laid in the late 1800s
and now are crumbling. We could be
upgrading right now—creating good
jobs and investing in our future.

—*elizabethwarren.com, "Priorities"*

Minimum wage workers haven't
gotten a raise in seven years,
and today nearly two-thirds of
minimum wage workers are women.
Mothers of very young children
disproportionately work low-wage
jobs in every state in the country.
A minimum wage job no longer
keeps a mother and baby above the
poverty line, yet Republicans continue
to block legislation to raise the
minimum wage.

—*Blog post, May 2014*

ON HER CHARACTER

—⁓—

I'm a wife, a mother, and a grandmother. For nearly all my life, I would have said I'm a teacher, but I guess I really can't say that anymore. Now I'd have to introduce myself as a United States senator, though I still feel a small jolt of surprise whenever I say that.

—A Fighting Chance

The word's out: I'm a woman and I'm going to have trouble backing off on that. I am what I am. I'll go out and talk to people about what's happening to their families, and when I do that, I'm a mother. I'm a grandmother.

—*The Daily Beast, October 2011*

Like a lot of you, I grew up in a family on the ragged edge of the middle class. My daddy sold carpeting and ended up as a maintenance man. After he had a heart attack, my mom worked the phones at Sears so we could hang on to our house. My three brothers all served in the military. One was career. The second worked a good union job in construction. The third started a small business.

—*Democratic National Convention, September 2012*

Me, I was waiting tables at 13 and married at 19. I graduated from public schools and taught elementary school. I have a wonderful husband, two great children, and three beautiful grandchildren. And I'm grateful, down to my toes, for every opportunity that America gave me.

—*Democratic National Convention, September 2012*

My daddy and I were both afraid of being poor, really poor. His response was never to talk about money or what might happen if it ran out—never ever ever. My response was to study contracts, finance, and, most of all, economic failure, to learn everything I could.

—A Fighting Chance

[Progressives] stand for small businesses, and for the millions of people who work every day to build a better future. And we stand for accountability and a level playing field so no one steals your purse on Main Street or your pension on Wall Street.

—*Remarks to Netroots Nation, June 2012*

"I came to the United States Senate late in life," she said. I didn't shape my life around how I could run for office and how I could have the maximum number of donors or allies. I came as a continuation of the consumer work I had done for 25 years. That work was the outsider's work.

—*The* New York Times, *April 2014*

Appendix A:
Opinions on Elizabeth Warren

—᠁—

She's your typical Oklahoma-born daughter of a carpet salesman and Sears worker who went on to become a state debating champion, attended public college, got married young, had kids early, graduated from law school while taking care of a toddler, earned a teaching position at Harvard Law School, and finally headed to Washington as the plainspoken voice of people getting crushed by so many predatory lenders and underregulated banks.

—*Brian McGrory, Boston.com*

In November 2008, Warren received a call from Senator Harry Reid. Lehman Brothers had collapsed two months before; A.I.G.'s bailout had just been upped to $150 billion, and Congress had passed TARP. Reid asked Warren to head the congressional panel overseeing the $700 billion bailout. The job was vague, with no clear goals, but Warren would turn it into a tough, prosecutorial committee.

—*Suzanna Andrews*, Vanity Fair

In a sense, says Barney Frank, the C.F.P.B. and Warren had become "a symbol" in a broader battle that was partly ideological. The anti-government, free-market, unregulated-business-as-the-savior-of-America sentiment of the Republican Party today, assisted by Wall Street's campaign donations, dovetailed perfectly with the interests of the country's banking Goliaths. To a degree, the attitude regarding Warren, Frank says, was "How dare this woman criticize the free-enterprise system?"

—Vanity Fair

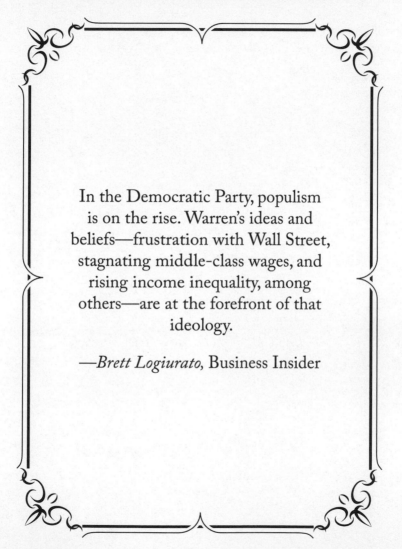

In the Democratic Party, populism is on the rise. Warren's ideas and beliefs—frustration with Wall Street, stagnating middle-class wages, and rising income inequality, among others—are at the forefront of that ideology.

—*Brett Logiurato,* Business Insider

A professor who spent most of her career teaching law students about bankruptcy, Warren is an unlikely icon for the Che Guevara T-shirt-wearing set.

—*Amy Chozick, the* New York Times

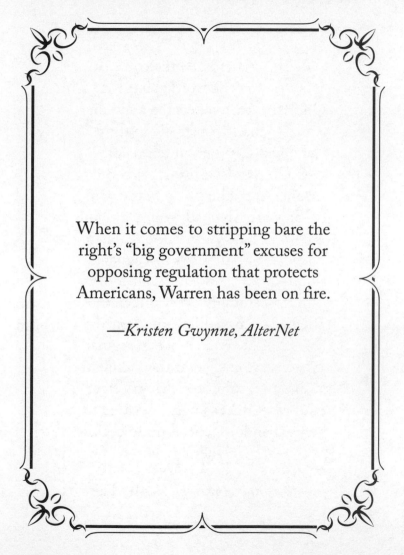

When it comes to stripping bare the right's "big government" excuses for opposing regulation that protects Americans, Warren has been on fire.

—*Kristen Gwynne, AlterNet*

As she crisscrossed the country, spreading the word about the C.F.P.B., Warren became a familiar face to many, especially to those who had seen her on television—on CNBC, Real Time with Bill Maher, and The Daily Show with Jon Stewart. She had gained millions of supporters. With her passionate defense of America's beleaguered middle class, under assault today from seemingly every direction, she had become like a modern-day Mr. Smith, giving voice to regular citizens astonished at the failure of Washington to protect Main Street—and what increasingly appeared to be its abandonment of middle-class America.

—*Suzanna Andrews,* Vanity Fair

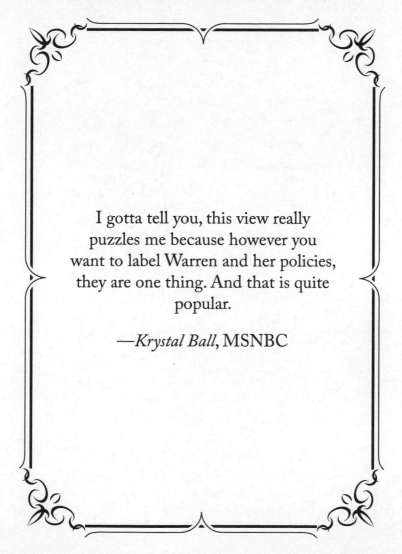

I gotta tell you, this view really puzzles me because however you want to label Warren and her policies, they are one thing. And that is quite popular.

—*Krystal Ball*, MSNBC

Geithner would never criticize Warren publicly—and indeed, as a Treasury spokesperson says, he "has expressed his support and admiration for Professor Warren many times"— but few people in Washington doubted that he remained opposed to her candidacy. To at least one person who saw them in meetings together it appeared that "he looked down on her for no apparent or justifiable reason." As for Warren, if one mentions the video "Elizabeth Warren Makes Timmy Geithner Squirm," she says nothing, but an impish smile crosses her face.

—*Suzanna Andrews*, Vanity Fair

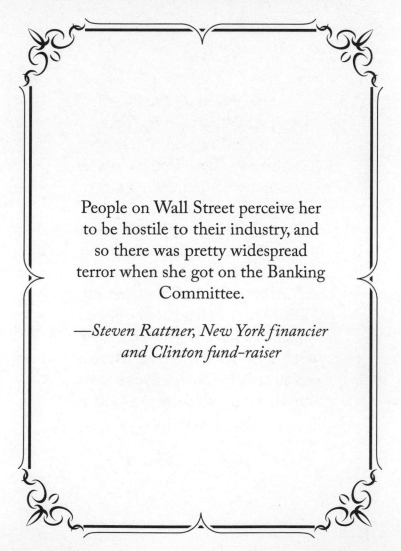

People on Wall Street perceive her to be hostile to their industry, and so there was pretty widespread terror when she got on the Banking Committee.

—*Steven Rattner, New York financier and Clinton fund-raiser*

Her track record on standing up [against] Wall Street is a pretty good one and anyone who upsets the American Right in the way that Warren does is generally a great bet. Shortly after announcing her candidacy, she was confronted by an irate audience member at a speech who accused her of being a "whore" aligned with the OWS movement. YES! This ringing endorsement solidified what any self-respecting leftist already knew: saying Warren was a better candidate than Brown was like saying it's colder in January than it is in July.

—*Michael Arria, CounterPunch*

But in seizing on issues animating her party's base—the influence of big banks, soaring student loan debt and the widening gulf between the wealthy and the working class—Ms. Warren is challenging the centrist economic approach that has been the de facto Democratic policy since President Bill Clinton and his fellow moderates took control of the party two decades ago.

—*Jonathan Martin, the* New York Times

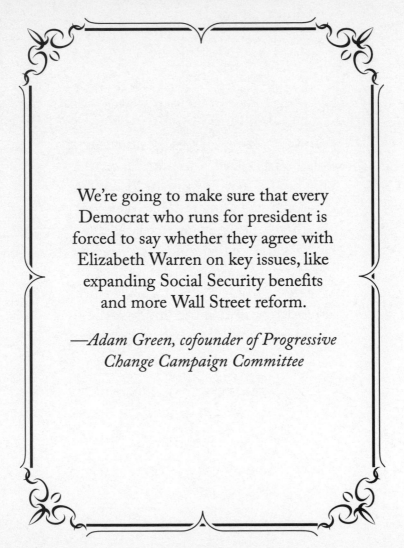

We're going to make sure that every Democrat who runs for president is forced to say whether they agree with Elizabeth Warren on key issues, like expanding Social Security benefits and more Wall Street reform.

—Adam Green, cofounder of Progressive Change Campaign Committee

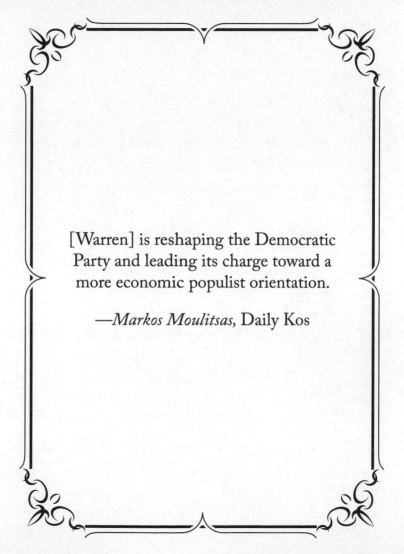

[Warren] is reshaping the Democratic
Party and leading its charge toward a
more economic populist orientation.

—*Markos Moulitsas,* Daily Kos

Elizabeth Warren has been a driving force behind the creation of the consumer financial protection bureau, and we have worked very closely with her over the past year and a half to make that idea a reality. Given her strong leadership on consumer protection, Secretary Geithner believes that Elizabeth Warren is exceptionally well qualified to lead the new bureau, and, ultimately, that's a decision the President will have to make.

—*Treasury spokesman*

"America's middle class is under attack," "The game is deliberately rigged" and "Politics so often felt dirty to me," . . . are the flash points, after all, that have become central to the Democratic Party and a White House grappling with how to address income inequality. The anti-Wall Street sentiment for which Warren is the poster girl led to the Occupy Wall Street movement and helped elect Bill de Blasio as the mayor of New York.

—*Amy Chozick, the* New York Times

Warren, a onetime schoolteacher who became a professor, is still more schoolmarmy than professorial—and I mean that in a good way. (She reminds me of my beloved fourth-grade teacher, Mrs. Summerskill.) When Warren is on her game, she's almost as good as Hillary's husband (or Nancy's) at *'splaining stuff* in plain language, above all when she's talking about her signature issue, financial reform.

—*Hendrik HertzBerg,* The New Yorker

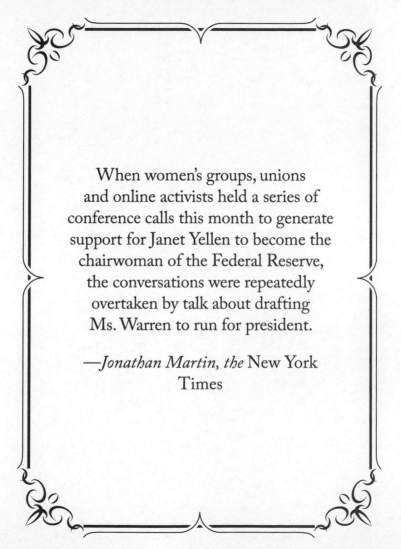

When women's groups, unions and online activists held a series of conference calls this month to generate support for Janet Yellen to become the chairwoman of the Federal Reserve, the conversations were repeatedly overtaken by talk about drafting Ms. Warren to run for president.

—*Jonathan Martin, the* New York Times

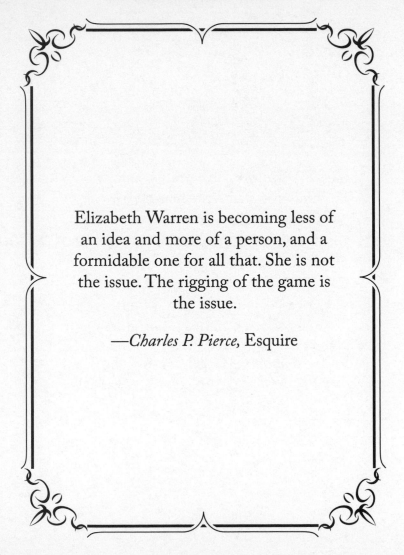

Elizabeth Warren is becoming less of an idea and more of a person, and a formidable one for all that. She is not the issue. The rigging of the game is the issue.

—*Charles P. Pierce*, Esquire

The reaction to Warren in the room made clear that if she winds up in the Senate in 2013, she will immediately become part of the 2016 Democratic presidential conversation. But, the heat with which Warren delivered her speech made us wonder that it might not make it slightly harder for her to get to the Senate this fall.

—*Chris Cillizza, the* Washington Post

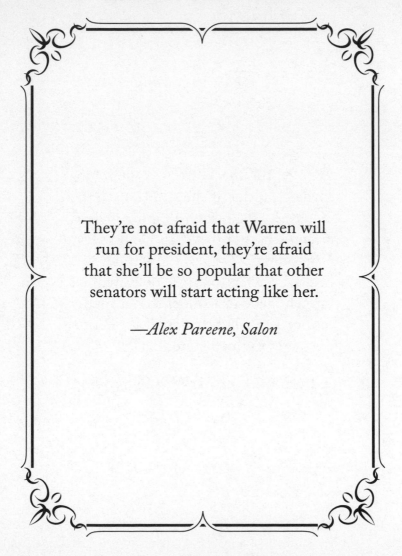

They're not afraid that Warren will run for president, they're afraid that she'll be so popular that other senators will start acting like her.

—*Alex Pareene, Salon*

Elizabeth Warren has pledged she will not seek the White House in 2016, but that has not stopped diehard Warren boosters from promoting her political profile in presidential primary states, saying she is best positioned to push the Democratic Party to the left.

—*Noah Bierman, the* Boston Globe

Ms. Warren . . . said in an interview
that she was not interested in seeking
the presidency. And despite talk
of a draft movement among some
activists, it is difficult to imagine her
taking on former Secretary of State
Hillary Rodham Clinton.

—*Jonathan Martin, the* New York
Times

In addition to being strongly identified with the party's populist wing, any candidate who challenged Clinton would need several key assets. The candidate would almost certainly have to be a woman, given Democrats' desire to make history again. She would have to amass huge piles of money with relatively little effort. Above all, she would have to awaken in Democratic voters an almost evangelical passion. As it happens, there is precisely such a person. Her name is Elizabeth Warren.

—*Noam Scheiber*, New Republic

—ⅿⅿ—

If you talk to leading progressives these days, you'll be sure to hear this message: The Democratic Party should embrace the economic populism of New York Mayor-elect Bill de Blasio and Massachusetts Sen. Elizabeth Warren. Such economic populism, they argue, should be the guiding star for Democrats heading into 2016. Nothing would be more disastrous for Democrats.

—*Jon Cowan and Jim Kessler,*
the Wall Street Journal

A group called "Third Way" criticized Warren. Warren apparently suspected that Third Way's criticism of her was funded by banks. So she wrote a letter to bank CEOs demanding they disclose which political groups they're funding. Warren sits on the Senate Committee on Banking, Housing, and Urban Affairs. She's basically telling the entities whose livelihood her committee controls to stop criticizing her. This is bullying—and it's the best argument for allowing companies and individuals to anonymously criticize politicians.

—*Ben White, Politico*

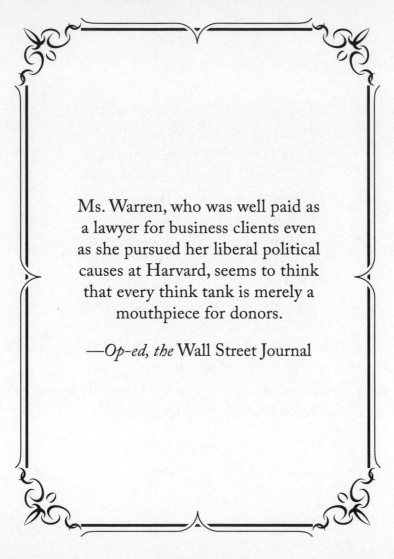

Ms. Warren, who was well paid as a lawyer for business clients even as she pursued her liberal political causes at Harvard, seems to think that every think tank is merely a mouthpiece for donors.

—*Op-ed, the* Wall Street Journal

What I've tried to do is find liberal middle-of-the-road Republicans and Democrats. In the Senate, Scott Brown, who single-handedly stopped the right-to-carry bill. You can question whether he's too conservative. You can question, in my mind, whether [Warren is] God's gift to regulation, close the banks and get rid of corporate profits, and we'd all bring socialism back, or the U.S.S.R.

—Former NY Mayor Bloomberg on support of Scott Brown over Elizabeth Warren

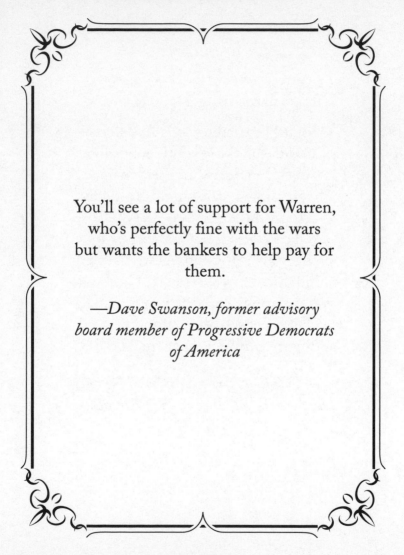

You'll see a lot of support for Warren, who's perfectly fine with the wars but wants the bankers to help pay for them.

—*Dave Swanson, former advisory board member of Progressive Democrats of America*

[Warren] seems to have fallen for the balance budget meme, when the proper role of government fiscal policy is to accommodate the actions of the private sector, meaning households and business. Households want to save for retirement and emergencies, and the tacit assumption is business invests household savings. Unless a country is running a trade surplus, and the U.S. is not in that category, the government needs to accommodate the desire of the private sector to save by deficit spending. Otherwise wages fall and the economy contracts, and that makes the debt to GDP ratio worse.

—*Yves Smith (Susan Webber), Naked Capitalism*

Criticism of Warren's warmongering has been virtually nonexistent and millions of dollars have poured into her campaign, without caveats. . . . The transcendent issue is now the economy and, as good as Warren is on that, her blemishes on war factor into her perception of the dilemma.

—*Michael Arria, CounterPunch*

If you are Native, there is no doubt, and if one has to research to try and ascertain if they are Native American, I would have great concerns with that and I think naturally I would just wonder if that was a vehicle she would want to use to her benefit. If that is the case, shame on her.

—*Rob Capriccioso, Indian Country Today*

I have no idea whether Senator Warren doesn't understand that distinction, or disagrees with it, or finds it politically convenient to point to profits being made by the government off student loans, even though they're not real.

—*Matthew Chingos*

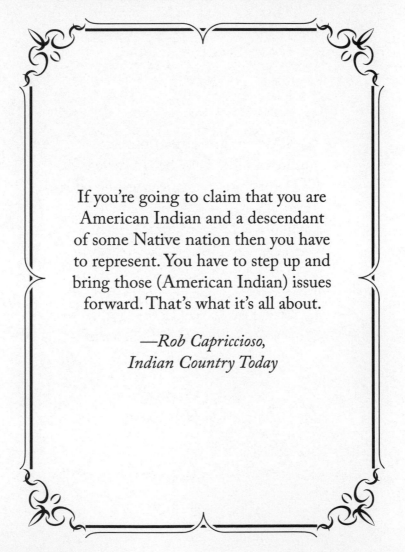

If you're going to claim that you are American Indian and a descendant of some Native nation then you have to represent. You have to step up and bring those (American Indian) issues forward. That's what it's all about.

—*Rob Capriccioso,*
Indian Country Today

So, when prominent public luminaries like Elizabeth Warren, the Democratic nominee for Senate from Massachusetts, popularize a problematic interpretation of racial legacy as an abstract constructs assumed at will, they hasten a Native cultural corrosion originally instigated by formal early twentieth-century American government policies of acculturation.

—*Cole DeLaune,*
Indian Country Today

NOTES

NOTES

NOTES

NOTES

NOTES

NOTES

NOTES

NOTES

NOTES

NOTES

NOTES